© **Classic Publishing**

Please feel free to share your feedback of using this journal on the Amazon page by leaving us a review, or just contact us at our email address: **ClassicPublishingAmazon@gmail.com**

By leaving your opinion, you help us make our products better for you to enjoy, so thank you!

Follow **@HikingAmbience** across all platforms for hiking-related content.

Table of Contents

8. Essential equipment ....
10. Mountains I've climbed ....
13. Encountered wildlife ....
16. My hiking bucket list ....
19. World map ....
20. How to journal ....
24. Crown of the Continent ....
25. ....
28. Ancient trail in Europe ....
29. ....
32. Lowest point in North America ....
33. ....
36. K2 in winter ....
37. ....
40. First European in North America ....
41. ....
44. Sacred Buddhist monastery in the Himalayas ....
45. ....
48. Supervolcano eruptions ....

49. ....

52. The Great Wall of China ....

53. ....

56. Seen from space ....

57. ....

60. Reinhold Andreas Messner ....

61. ....

64. Longest cave system ....

65. ....

68. Munro Bagging ....

69. ....

72. Most famous arch ....

73. ....

76. Blown up mountain in Italy ....

77. ....

80. Oldest hiking trail ....

81. ....

84. Samurai training grounds ....

85. ....

88. Lighthouse in the middle of desert ....

89. ....

92. Mountains painted blue ....

93. ....

96. Longest hiking-only footpath ....
97. ....
100. The Land of the Bigfeet ....
101. ....
104. Need for adrenaline ....
105. ....
108. The Stairway To Heaven ....
109. ....
112. General Sherman ....
113. ....
116. Real-world Indiana Jones ....
117. ....
120. Deepest lake in the United States ....
121. ....

Essential Equipment

Every hike begins with preparing the right equipment - clothes, food, and other needed accessories. Create a personalized checklist with gear for your adventures to make sure you've got all the essentials.

- [ ]
- [ ]
- [ ]
- [ ]
- [ ]
- [ ]
- [ ]
- [ ]
- [ ]
- [ ]
- [ ]
- [ ]
- [ ]
- [ ]
- [ ]
- [ ]
- [ ]

Mountains I've Climbed

Keep a record of all the peaks you've summited. Write in the name of the mountain and the date of when you completed that hike. You can also include the journal page number for where you've written about that trip.

MOUNTAIN NAME: .... **DATE:** ....
(log page) ......

MOUNTAIN NAME: .... **DATE:** ....
(log page) ......

MOUNTAIN NAME: .... **DATE:** ....
(log page) ......

MOUNTAIN NAME: .... **DATE:** ....
(log page) ......

MOUNTAIN NAME: .... **DATE:** ....
(log page) ......

MOUNTAIN NAME: .... **DATE:** ....
(log page) ......

MOUNTAIN NAME: .... **DATE:** ....
(log page) ......

(log page)	MOUNTAIN NAME:	DATE: ....
(log page)	MOUNTAIN NAME:	DATE: ....
(log page)	MOUNTAIN NAME:	DATE: ....
(log page)	MOUNTAIN NAME:	DATE: ....
(log page)	MOUNTAIN NAME:	DATE: ....
(log page)	MOUNTAIN NAME:	DATE: ....
(log page)	MOUNTAIN NAME:	DATE: ....
(log page)	MOUNTAIN NAME:	DATE: ....
(log page)	MOUNTAIN NAME:	DATE: ....
(log page)	MOUNTAIN NAME:	DATE: ....

(log page)	MOUNTAIN NAME:	DATE:
(log page)	MOUNTAIN NAME:	DATE:
(log page)	MOUNTAIN NAME:	DATE:
(log page)	MOUNTAIN NAME:	DATE:
(log page)	MOUNTAIN NAME:	DATE:
(log page)	MOUNTAIN NAME:	DATE:
(log page)	MOUNTAIN NAME:	DATE:
(log page)	MOUNTAIN NAME:	DATE:
(log page)	MOUNTAIN NAME:	DATE:
(log page)	MOUNTAIN NAME:	DATE:

Encountered Wildlife

Write down every animal you encounter during your hikes. You can also enter many locations and log pages / dates for just one species.

Date seen: ....
ANIMAL: LOG PAGE:
....
LOCATION:
....

Date seen: ....
ANIMAL: LOG PAGE:
....
LOCATION:
....

Date seen: ....
ANIMAL: LOG PAGE:
....
LOCATION:
....

Date seen: ....
ANIMAL: LOG PAGE:
....
LOCATION:
....

Date seen: ....

ANIMAL: .... LOG PAGE: ....

LOCATION: ....

....

Date seen: ....

ANIMAL: .... LOG PAGE: ....

LOCATION: ....

....

Date seen: ....

ANIMAL: .... LOG PAGE: ....

LOCATION: ....

....

Date seen: ....

ANIMAL: .... LOG PAGE: ....

LOCATION: ....

....

Date seen: ....

ANIMAL: .... LOG PAGE: ....

LOCATION: ....

....

Date seen:
ANIMAL: LOG PAGE:
LOCATION:

Date seen:
ANIMAL: LOG PAGE:
LOCATION:

Date seen:
ANIMAL: LOG PAGE:
LOCATION:

Date seen:
ANIMAL: LOG PAGE:
LOCATION:

Date seen:
ANIMAL: LOG PAGE:
LOCATION:

My Hiking Bucket List

On this page you can list all the trails you'd like to explore, mountains you plan to climb, or any other location you want to reach. Once you've achieved the assumed goal on this list, you can check it off.

- [ ] ....
- [ ] ....
- [ ] ....
- [ ] ....
- [ ] ....
- [ ] ....
- [ ] ....
- [ ] ....
- [ ] ....

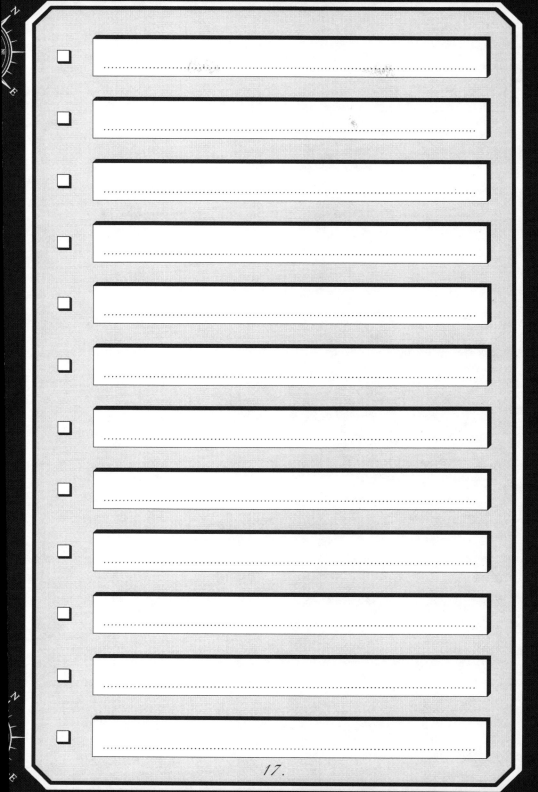

> "A journey of a thousand miles begins with a single step."
>
> - Lao Tzu -

How to Journal

The next pages will explain and show, with examples, how you can fill up the spaces in each log of the journal. Every entry consists of four pages.

The first includes a short story or fun fact related to hiking to get you inspired, inform you of some truly wonderful places to visit, or give you something extra in addition to the usual journaling from the trail. You can also find an animated version of those stories you read below on **@HikingAmbience** social media.

The second page is all about quick information for the trail – name, region, distance, duration, facilities, weather, etc.

The third is for listing your equipment, documenting the exact route you've taken, and notes for every observation about the hike: waypoints, wildlife encounters, etc. There's more room for a more detailed report of the trip.

The last, fourth page is a summary of your adventure – a place to paste a photo from the trail (optionally, instead of pasting a picture, you can draw something or use this space for extra notes), write down the pros and cons of the hike, rate the difficulty, and give an overall rating.

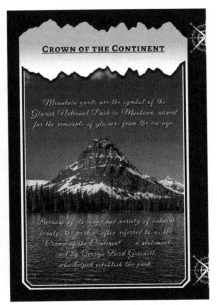

As mentioned earlier, each four-paged entry begins with a story or fun fact from the hiking world which will give you some cool trivia to talk about in casual conversation with your hiking buddies.

For an even more engaging version of those stories, you can visit my social media profiles, where all stories will be published as short, animated videos (across all platforms, so watch wherever is most convenient for you). Just type in **@HikingAmbience** or scan the QR codes listed below to go to my profile on your chosen app.

 @HikingAmbience

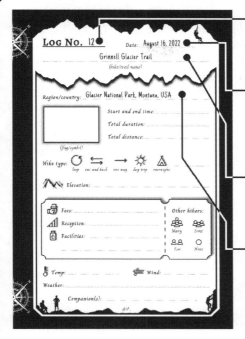

Write in the number for each entry. If this is an additional copy of the journal, you can continue numbering your hikes from where you left off.

Enter the date of your hike. If your adventure is going to take more than one day, you could write a date range or just record each day in an individual log for more journaling space.

Record the official name of the trail you are about to take – or provide one that will be clear and meaningful for you.

Here you write the region where you took your hike. You can be very specific in your description by putting the name of a park, mountain range, canyon, river, etc., then giving the name of the state, and lastly country. Alternatively, go broad and record only the name of the country (or even continent!) of the trail - whatever you seem fit.

A place to print, paste, or draw anything that will remind you of the region or specific location where you had your adventure. It could be the emblem or a symbol of the national park (for Glacier National Park it could be a mountain goat). If you want to remember the state/province of a given country, you could go with the flag like in the example page, which shows the flag of the state of Montana. You can be even broader and paste the flag of the entire country!

Write the time you started your journey and the time it ended. If you decide to record a two- or three-day hike in one log, you can also give the dates next to the hours.

Sum up how much time the trail took you to beat.

How much distance did you cover? Express it in whatever unit of measurement you use – miles, kilometers.

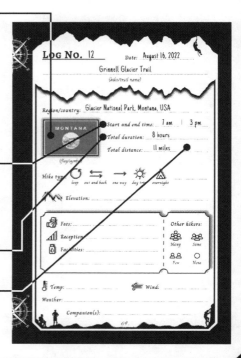

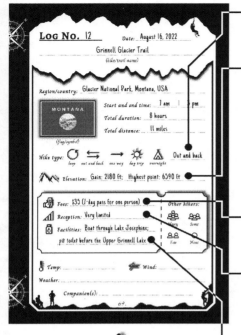

Record the hike type you went on. If your hike doesn't match any of the specific types, you can name it too.

Journal how much elevation you gained, how much you lost, the height of the highest point on the trail, or maybe even the height of the starting point. The example page shows no elevation loss because it's an "out and back" type of hike, meaning the elevation loss value will be the same as the gain.

If there are any fees you need to pay for entering certain areas, parking, etc., record them here.

How well did your phone and GPS work? Was there any reception? Write down any places where you found a decent signal.

Write about facilities you came across the trail – freshwater availability, toilets, campfires, shelters, etc.

Color the graphics or underline text to represent how many other people were on the trail.

Was it windy on your trip? Describe it like in the example page or be more precise and write down miles/kilometers per hour.

Enter the range of temperatures you encountered on your hike. Be meticulous and give each hour a specific temperature, put the average, or just express it in phrase form like "hot", "cold", etc.

Was it a sunny or cloudy day? Maybe you were caught up in rain or snow. Here is where you report all the atmospheric conditions from the trail.

Journal whether you had a solo hike or with some friends. If there were others, write their names.

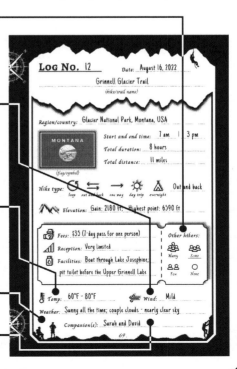

List the equipment you took on that particular adventure. You can get really detailed, giving the exact model and brand like in the example page, or write more generally and record only item names.

Document the course of the route you took. Record only the trail names you're going through or include some more information like cardinal directions, distinct waypoints, etc.

Journal all your observations and feelings from the hike. How was it and what were the highlights of that journey? Have you encountered any wildlife? Is there anything worth remembering for the next time? Here you can write it all down.

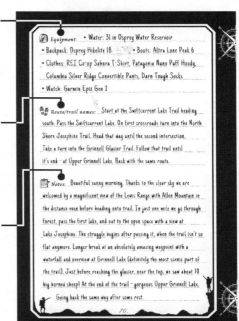

A place to print and paste your photo from the trip – there's enough space for a popular picture, size 4x6 inch (10x15 cm), like in the example page. You can also include a drawing if you'd prefer that. Or, if you really love journaling and the designated spaces turned out to be too short for you, you can use this extra page for more writing.

Any pros of the hike you took? Write them down.

Any cons of the hike you took? Write them down too.

Rate the difficulty of the hike by coloring the right number of stars.

What's the final verdict and rating for your hike? Color the right number of stars.

CROWN OF THE CONTINENT

Mountain goats are the symbol of the Glacier National Park in Montana, named for the remnants of glaciers from the ice age.

Because of its scope and variety of natural beauty, the park is often referred to as the "Crown of the Continent" – a statement said by George Bird Grinnell, who helped establish the park.

Log No. _____   Date: ....

....
(hike/trail name)

Region/country: ....

(flag/symbol)

Start and end time: .... | ....

Total duration: ....

Total distance: ....

Hike type: loop   out and back   one way   day trip   overnight

Elevation: ....

Fees: ....
Reception: ....
Facilities: ....
....

Other hikers:
Many   Some
Few   None

Temp: ....   Wind: ....

Weather: ....

Companion(s): ....

25.

Equipment: ....

....

....

....

....

Route/trail names: ....

....

....

....

....

Notes: ....

....

....

....

....

....

....

....

(photo/drawing/notes)

- Pros: ....
- Cons: ....

Difficulty: ☆☆☆☆☆   Overall rating: ☆☆☆☆☆

Ancient trail in Europe

The Via Francigena is an ancient trail in Europe running from the cathedral city of Canterbury, England, through France and Switzerland, and all the way to Rome, Italy.

Pilgrims travel this trail to see tombs of Saint Peter and Paul.

Log No. _____   Date: ....

....
(hike/trail name)

Region/country: ....

(flag/symbol)

Start and end time: .... | ....

Total duration: ....

Total distance: ....

Hike type: ↻ loop   ⇄ out and back   → one way   ☼ day trip   ⛺ overnight   ....

Elevation: ....

Fees: ....

Reception: ....

Facilities: ....
....

Other hikers:

Many   Some

Few   None

Temp: ....   Wind: ....

Weather: ....

Companion(s): ....

Equipment: ....
....
....
....
....

Route/trail names: ....
....
....
....
....

Notes: ....
....
....
....
....
....
....
....

(photo/drawing/notes)

- Pros: ....
- Cons: ....

Difficulty: ☆☆☆☆☆   Overall rating: ☆☆☆☆☆

Lowest Point in North America

You can go for a hike to California's Death Valley National Park to see the lowest point in North America – the Badwater Basin, with a depth of around 282 ft (86m) below sea level.

Thousands of years ago there was a large inland sea in that area but, over time, the water evaporated completely.

Log No. _____   Date: ....

....
(hike/trail name)

Region/country: ....

(flag/symbol)

Start and end time: .... | ....

Total duration: ....

Total distance: ....

Hike type: ⟲ loop   ⇄ out and back   → one way   ☀ day trip   ⛺ overnight   ....

Elevation: ....

Fees: ....
Reception: ....
Facilities: ....
....

Other hikers:
- Many
- Some
- Few
- None

Temp: ....   Wind: ....

Weather: ....

Companion(s): ....

Equipment: ....

....

....

....

....

Route/trail names: ....

....

....

....

....

Notes: ....

....

....

....

....

....

....

....

....

(photo/drawing/notes)

- Pros: ....
- Cons: ....

Difficulty: ☆☆☆☆☆   Overall rating: ☆☆☆☆☆

K2 IN WINTER

K2 is the second-highest mountain on Earth but, due its extreme and harsh conditions in winter, was not reached during that season till January of 2021, when a team of ten Nepali climbers made history by summiting the mountain in winter.

Log No. _____

Date: ....

....
(hike/trail name)

Region/country: ....

Start and end time: ....

Total duration: ....

Total distance: ....

(flag/symbol)

Hike type: loop   out and back   one way   day trip   overnight   ....

Elevation: ....

Fees: ....

Reception: ....

Facilities: ....

....

Other hikers:
Many   Some
Few   None

Temp: ....   Wind: ....

Weather: ....

Companion(s): ....

37.

Equipment:

Route/trail names:

Notes:

(photo/drawing/notes)

- Pros: ....
- Cons: ....

Difficulty: ☆☆☆☆☆   Overall rating: ☆☆☆☆☆

First European in North America

It is speculated that Leif Erikson, Norse explorer, was actually the first European to set foot on the continental North America approximately 500 years before Christopher Columbus.

There is also a hypothesis that he built a settlement with his crew in today's Newfoundland, Canada.

Log No. _____   Date: ....

....
(hike/trail name)

Region/country: ....

(flag/symbol)

Start and end time: .... | ....

Total duration: ....

Total distance: ....

Hike type:
loop   out and back   one way   day trip   overnight

 Elevation: ....

 Fees: ....

Reception: ....

Facilities: ....
....

Other hikers:

Many   Some

Few   None

Temp: ....   Wind: ....

Weather: ....

Companion(s): ....

41.

Equipment:

Route/trail names:

Notes:

(photo/drawing/notes)

- Pros: ....
- Cons: ....

Difficulty: ☆☆☆☆☆　　Overall rating: ☆☆☆☆☆

SACRED BUDDHIST MONASTERY IN THE HIMALAYAS

The Himalayas is the mountain range that has many of the highest peaks of the planet and is also known for numerous distinct landmarks to hike to.

One of the most iconic, due to its amazing localization at the side of the mountain, is the so-called Tiger's Nest in the Kingdom of Bhutan.

Legends say that Guru Rinpoche, Buddhism master, flew on the back of a tigress to the location of today's monastery and meditated there.

Log No. _____   Date: ....

....
(hike/trail name)

Region/country: ....

(flag/symbol)

Start and end time: .... | ....

Total duration: ....

Total distance: ....

Hike type: ◯ loop   ⇄ out and back   → one way   ☀ day trip   △ overnight   ....

Elevation: ....

Fees: ....

Reception: ....

Facilities: ....

....

Other hikers:
Many   Some
Few   None

Temp: ....   Wind: ....

Weather: ....

Companion(s): ....

45.

Equipment: ....
....
....
....
....

Route/trail names: ....
....
....
....
....

Notes: ....
....
....
....
....
....
....
....
....

(photo/drawing/notes)

Pros: ....

Cons: ....

Difficulty: ☆☆☆☆☆   Overall rating: ☆☆☆☆☆

SUPERVOLCANO ERUPTIONS

Famous geysers in the Yellowstone National Park are caused by the activity of the Yellowstone supervolcano that lies underneath the park.

There have been three super-eruptions of the volcano, the most recent occurring approximately 640,000 years ago.

Log No. _____   Date: ....

....
(hike/trail name)

Region/country: ....

(flag/symbol)

Start and end time: .... | ....

Total duration: ....

Total distance: ....

Hike type: ○ loop   ⇆ out and back   → one way   ☀ day trip   ⛺ overnight ....

Elevation: ....

Fees: ....

Reception: ....

Facilities: ....
....

Other hikers:

Many   Some

Few   None

Temp: ....   Wind: ....

Weather: ....

Companion(s): ....

49.

Equipment: ....

....
....
....
....

Route/trail names: ....

....
....
....
....

Notes: ....

....
....
....
....
....
....
....
....

(photo/drawing/notes)

- **Pros:** ....
- **Cons:** ....

Difficulty: ☆☆☆☆☆   **Overall rating:** ☆☆☆☆☆

The Great Wall of China

China is home to many breathtaking hiking trails. The Great Wall, with its stunning views, is surely one of the most iconic.

The first parts of the wall were built over 2,000 years ago and were created for the imposition of duties on goods, to control immigration and emigration, but mostly as protection against nomadic groups from the Eurasian Steppe.

Log No. _____

Date: ....

....
(hike/trail name)

Region/country: ....

(flag/symbol)

Start and end time: .... | ....

Total duration: ....

Total distance: ....

Hike type:
- ↻ loop
- ⇄ out and back
- → one way
- ☀ day trip
- ⛺ overnight

⛰ Elevation: ....

Fees: ....

Reception: ....

Facilities: ....
....

Other hikers:
- Many
- Some
- Few
- None

🌡 Temp: .... 💨 Wind: ....

Weather: ....

Companion(s): ....

53

Equipment: ....
....
....
....
....

Route/trail names: ....
....
....
....
....

Notes: ....
....
....
....
....
....
....
....

(photo/drawing/notes)

- Pros: ....
- Cons: ....

Difficulty: ☆☆☆☆☆   Overall rating: ☆☆☆☆☆

SEEN FROM SPACE

The Grand Canyon National Park is one of the most beautiful places to hike in the United States.

It has the most extensive canyon system in the world. In fact, it's so big and its shape is so distinctive that it can be seen even from space.

Log No. _____   Date: ....

.... (hike/trail name) ....

Region/country: ....

(flag/symbol)

Start and end time: ....
Total duration: ....
Total distance: ....

Hike type: loop   out and back   one way   day trip   overnight

Elevation: ....

Fees: ....
Reception: ....
Facilities: ....

Other hikers:
Many   Some
Few   None

Temp: ....   Wind: ....

Weather: ....

Companion(s): ....

57.

Equipment: ....

....
....
....
....

Route/trail names: ....

....
....
....
....

Notes: ....

....
....
....
....
....
....
....
....

(photo/drawing/notes)

Pros: ....

Cons: ....

Difficulty: ☆☆☆☆☆   **Overall rating:** ☆☆☆☆☆

Reinhold Andreas Messner

Reinhold Andreas Messner is the first man that summited all fourteen so-called "Eight-thousanders" – mountains that are more than 8,000m (26,247 ft above sea level) in height.

Log No. _____

Date: ....

....
(hike/trail name)

Region/country: ....

(flag/symbol)

Start and end time: ....

Total duration: ....

Total distance: ....

Hike type:
loop out and back one way day trip overnight ....

Elevation: ....

Fees: ....

Reception: ....

Facilities: ....
....

Other hikers:

Many   Some

Few   None

Temp: ....   Wind: ....

Weather: ....

Companion(s): ....

61.

Equipment: ....
....
....
....
....

Route/trail names: ....
....
....
....
....

Notes: ....
....
....
....
....
....
....
....
....

(photo/drawing/notes)

- Pros: ....
- Cons: ....

Difficulty: ☆☆☆☆☆   Overall rating: ☆☆☆☆☆

Longest cave system

If hiking breathtaking mountain tops, picturesque valleys, or rushing rivers got a little bit repetitive, then you should visit Kentucky's Mammoth Cave National Park, which contains the longest cave system known in the world.

These natural tunnels go for over 400 miles (640 km) and yet, even to this day, new passages are still being discovered.

Log No. ....

Date: ....

....
(hike/trail name)

Region/country: ....

Start and end time: ....

Total duration: ....

Total distance: ....

(flag/symbol)

Hike type: ○ loop   ⇄ out and back   → one way   ☀ day trip   ⛺ overnight

Elevation: ....

Fees: ....

Reception: ....

Facilities: ....
....

Other hikers:
Many   Some
Few   None

Temp: ....   Wind: ....

Weather: ....

Companion(s): ....

Equipment: ....
....
....
....
....

Route/trail names: ....
....
....
....
....

Notes: ....
....
....
....
....
....
....
....

(photo/drawing/notes)

Pros: ....

Cons: ....

Difficulty: ☆☆☆☆☆   Overall rating: ☆☆☆☆☆

Munro Bagging

Besides great scotch whisky, Scotland is also known for its dramatic landscapes and the hiking opportunities that this diverse land creates.

For example, so-called Munro Bagging refers to hiking Munros.

Munros are mountains in Scotland over 3,000 ft (914m) in height and there are exactly 282 of them.

When you reach the summit, you've bagged a Munro.

Log No. _____

Date: ....

....
(hike/trail name)

Region/country: ....

Start and end time: .... | ....

Total duration: ....

Total distance: ....

(flag/symbol)

Hike type: loop   out and back   one way   day trip   overnight

Elevation: ....

Fees: ....

Reception: ....

Facilities: ....
....

Other hikers:
Many   Some
Few   None

Temp: ....   Wind: ....

Weather: ....

Companion(s): ....

Equipment: ....
....
....
....
....

Route/trail names: ....
....
....
....
....

Notes: ....
....
....
....
....
....
....
....

(photo/drawing/notes)

- Pros: ....
- Cons: ....

Difficulty: ☆☆☆☆☆   Overall rating: ☆☆☆☆☆

Most Famous Arch

You can go for a hike in the Arches National Park in Utah to see the iconic Delicate Arch, the most famous natural freestanding arch in the whole world known for its distinctive, dramatic shape.

Log No. _____

Date: ....

....
(hike/trail name)

Region/country: ....

(flag/symbol)

Start and end time: ....

Total duration: ....

Total distance: ....

Hike type: loop   out and back   one way   day trip   overnight   ....

Elevation: ....

Fees: ....

Reception: ....

Facilities: ....

....

Other hikers:

Many   Some

Few   None

Temp: ....   Wind: ....

Weather: ....

Companion(s): ....

73.

Equipment: ....
....
....
....
....

Route/trail names: ....
....
....
....
....

Notes: ....
....
....
....
....
....
....
....
....

(photo/drawing/notes)

- **Pros:** ....
- **Cons:** ....

Difficulty: ☆☆☆☆☆ **Overall rating:** ☆☆☆☆☆

Blown up mountain in Italy

The Alta Via trail in the Dolomites mountain range – that's the Italian part of the Alps – is considered one of the most beautiful long-distance hiking routes in the world.

During the hike you will pass Lagazuoi mountain, which is known for its tunnels from the First World War, when the Austro-Hungarian army fought the Italian army.

They were blowing each other up with mines, which led to the creations massive landslides at the foot of the mountain.

Today, you can explore those drilled tunnels inside the mountain.

Log No. _____

Date: ....

....
(hike/trail name)

Region/country: ....

(flag/symbol)

Start and end time: ....

Total duration: ....

Total distance: ....

Hike type: loop | out and back | one way | day trip | overnight

Elevation: ....

Fees: ....

Reception: ....

Facilities: ....

....

Other hikers:

Many | Some
Few | None

Temp: .... Wind: ....

Weather: ....

Companion(s): ....

77.

Equipment: ....

....

....

....

....

Route/trail names: ....

....

....

....

....

Notes: ....

....

....

....

....

....

....

....

(photo/drawing/notes)

- **Pros:** ....
- **Cons:** ....

Difficulty: ☆☆☆☆☆   **Overall rating:** ☆☆☆☆☆

Oldest Hiking Trail

The Crawford Path is considered the United States' oldest continuously maintained hiking trail.

It goes from the Crawford Notch pass to the summit of Mount Washington.

Log No. _____

Date: ....

....
(hike/trail name)

Region/country: ....

(flag/symbol)

Start and end time: ....

Total duration: ....

Total distance: ....

Hike type: ⟲ loop   ⇆ out and back   → one way   ☀ day trip   ⛺ overnight ....

⛰ Elevation: ....

Fees: ....

Reception: ....

Facilities: ....
....

Other hikers:
Many   Some
Few   None

🌡 Temp: ....   💨 Wind: ....

Weather: ....

Companion(s): ....

Equipment: ....
....
....
....
....
....

Route/trail names: ....
....
....
....
....

Notes: ....
....
....
....
....
....
....
....
....

(photo/drawing/notes)

- **Pros:** ....
- **Cons:** ....

Difficulty: ☆☆☆☆☆   **Overall rating:** ☆☆☆☆☆

Samurai Training Grounds

Mount Fuji is probably best known as an active volcano and the highest peak in Japan.

It has become the most iconic landmark of the country and a very popular hiking destination for travelers all around the world.

At the base of the mountain, however, are some restricted areas like Camp Fuji – terrains once used by legendary samurai warriors for training and now used by joint forces of Japan and the United States.

Log No. _____

Date: ....

....
(hike/trail name)

Region/country: ....

(flag/symbol)

Start and end time: ....

Total duration: ....

Total distance: ....

Hike type: ⟳ loop   ⇄ out and back   → one way   ☀ day trip   ⛺ overnight   ....

⛰ Elevation: ....

Fees: ....

Reception: ....

Facilities: ....

....

Other hikers:
- Many
- Some
- Few
- None

🌡 Temp: ....   💨 Wind: ....

Weather: ....

Companion(s): ....

85.

Equipment: ....

....

....

....

....

Route/trail names: ....

....

....

....

....

Notes: ....

....

....

....

....

....

....

....

....

(photo/drawing/notes)

- **Pros:** ....
- **Cons:** ....

Difficulty: ☆☆☆☆☆   **Overall rating:** ☆☆☆☆☆

Lighthouse in the Middle of Desert

Palo Duro Canyon, Texas, is the second-largest canyon in the United States.

Its name comes from Spanish and means "hard stick."

When looking for an adventure in this region, be sure to look up the hiking trail to the Lighthouse — the most famous rock formation in the canyon.

Log No. ....

Date: ....

....
(hike/trail name)

Region/country: ....

Start and end time: ....

Total duration: ....

Total distance: ....

(flag/symbol)

Hike type: ⟲ loop   ⇄ out and back   → one way   ☀ day trip   ⛺ overnight

Elevation: ....

Fees: ....

Reception: ....

Facilities: ....
....

Other hikers:

Many   Some

Few   None

Temp: ....   Wind: ....

Weather: ....

Companion(s): ....

Equipment: ....
....
....
....
....

Route/trail names: ....
....
....
....
....

Notes: ....
....
....
....
....
....
....
....
....

(photo/drawing/notes)

- **Pros:** ....
- **Cons:** ....

Difficulty: ☆☆☆☆☆   **Overall rating:** ☆☆☆☆☆

Mountains Painted Blue

The Sinai Trail is Egypt's first long-distance hiking trail.

It goes through mountains, deserts, oases, and landmarks like Mount Catherine — Egypt's highest mountain — or so-called Blue Mountain, where rocks were painted blue by an artist to celebrate the return of Sinai to Egypt after peace with Israel.

Log No. ....

Date: ....

....
(hike/trail name)

Region/country: ....

(flag/symbol)

Start and end time: .... | ....

Total duration: ....

Total distance: ....

Hike type: ☀ ⛺ ....
            loop   out and back   one way   day trip   overnight

 Elevation: ....

Fees: ....

Reception: ....

Facilities: ....
....

Other hikers:

Many   Some

Few   None

 Temp: ....   Wind: ....

Weather: ....

Companion(s): ....

93.

Equipment: ....
....
....
....
....

Route/trail names: ....
....
....
....
....

Notes: ....
....
....
....
....
....
....
....
....

(photo/drawing/notes)

Pros: ....

Cons: ....

Difficulty: ☆☆☆☆☆ Overall rating: ☆☆☆☆☆

LONGEST HIKING-ONLY FOOTPATH

The Appalachian Trail stretches for approximately 2,200 miles (3,540 km) and claims to be the longest hiking-only footpath in the world.

It's in the Eastern United States and goes through fourteen states.

Log No. _____

Date: ....

.... (hike/trail name) ....

Region/country: ....

(flag/symbol)

Start and end time: .... | ....

Total duration: ....

Total distance: ....

Hike type: ⟳ loop   ⇄ out and back   → one way   ☀ day trip   ⛺ overnight   ....

Elevation: ....

Fees: ....
Reception: ....
Facilities: ....
....

Other hikers:
Many   Some
Few   None

Temp: ....

Wind: ....

Weather: ....

Companion(s): ....

97.

Equipment: ....
....
....
....
....
....

Route/trail names: ....
....
....
....
....

Notes: ....
....
....
....
....
....
....
....

(photo/drawing/notes)

- **Pros:** ....
- **Cons:** ....

Difficulty: ☆☆☆☆☆   **Overall rating:** ☆☆☆☆☆

The Land of the Bigfeet

Portuguese explorer Ferdinand Magellan was the first European to set foot in the region of Patagonia.

It's likely best known for being home to the longest mountain range in the world – the Andes, with some incredible hike trails.

One of the stories about the origin of the name of the land comes through a Portuguese explorer meeting the native people, which he perceived as giants.

Thus, he named the region "patagones," or "Land of the Bigfeet."

Log No. _____

Date: ....

....
(hike/trail name)

Region/country: ....

Start and end time: ....

Total duration: ....

Total distance: ....

(flag/symbol)

Hike type: ⟲ loop   ⇄ out and back   → one way   ☀ day trip   ⛺ overnight

Elevation: ....

Fees: ....

Reception: ....

Facilities: ....

....

Other hikers:

Many   Some

Few   None

Temp: ....   Wind: ....

Weather: ....

Companion(s): ....

101.

Equipment: ....

....
....
....
....

Route/trail names: ....

....
....
....
....

Notes: ....

....
....
....
....
....
....
....

(photo/drawing/notes)

- **Pros:** ....
- **Cons:** ....

Difficulty: ☆☆☆☆☆   **Overall rating:** ☆☆☆☆☆

NEED FOR ADRENALINE

Hike alongside the Colorado River for some truly amazing views.

When you will feel the need for more of an adrenaline kick, the white water rafting spots on Colorado River are among the best in the world.

Log No. _____

Date: ....

....
(hike/trail name)

Region/country: ....

Start and end time: ....

Total duration: ....

Total distance: ....

(flag/symbol)

Hike type: loop   out and back   one way   day trip   overnight

Elevation: ....

Fees: ....

Reception: ....

Facilities: ....
....

Other hikers:
Many   Some
Few   None

Temp: ....   Wind: ....

Weather: ....

Companion(s): ....

Equipment: ....
....
....
....
....

Route/trail names: ....
....
....
....
....

Notes: ....
....
....
....
....
....
....
....
....

(photo/drawing/notes)

Pros: ....

Cons: ....

Difficulty: ☆☆☆☆☆   Overall rating: ☆☆☆☆☆

The Stairway To Heaven

When visiting China's epic hiking trails that go through numerous mountain temples or cliff paths which encircle the peaks, you can't forget about Tianmen Mountain, Tianmen Cave, and the 999 steps that take you there, known as Stairway to Heaven.

The cave, or so-called Gateway to Heaven, is the world's highest naturally formed arch and was created when one side of the mountain's cliff collapsed.

Log No. _____

Date: ....

....
(hike/trail name)

Region/country: ....

Start and end time: .... | ....

Total duration: ....

Total distance: ....

(flag/symbol)

Hike type: loop   out and back   one way   day trip   overnight

Elevation: ....

Fees: ....

Reception: ....

Facilities: ....

....

Other hikers:

Many   Some

Few   None

Temp: ....   Wind: ....

Weather: ....

Companion(s): ....

Equipment: ....
....
....
....
....

Route/trail names: ....
....
....
....
....

Notes: ....
....
....
....
....
....
....
....

(photo/drawing/notes)

- **Pros:** ....
- **Cons:** ....

Difficulty: ☆☆☆☆☆   **Overall rating:** ☆☆☆☆☆

GENERAL SHERMAN

If you're a tree fan,
you should go for a hike to the
Sequoia National Park in California,
home to the General Sherman,
the world's biggest tree
measured by volume.

It is approximately 275 ft (83m) tall,
36 ft (11m) in diameter at the base,
and 1,900 tons in weight.

Log No. _____   Date: ....

.... (hike/trail name) ....

Region/country: ....

Start and end time: .... | ....

Total duration: ....

Total distance: ....

(flag/symbol)

Hike type:
- loop
- out and back
- one way
- day trip
- overnight

Elevation: ....

Fees: ....
Reception: ....
Facilities: ....
....

Other hikers:
- Many
- Some
- Few
- None

Temp: ....   Wind: ....

Weather: ....

Companion(s): ....

113.

Equipment: ....

....
....
....
....

Route/trail names: ....

....
....
....
....

Notes: ....

....
....
....
....
....
....
....

(photo/drawing/notes)

Pros:
Cons:
Difficulty: ☆☆☆☆☆   Overall rating: ☆☆☆☆☆

Real-world Indiana Jones

Machu Picchu is a true wonder of the world which probably hangs on the bucket list of every hiker.

The discovery of this amazing site is credited to Hiram Bingham, who became one of the many sources of inspiration when George Lucas was creating the character of Indiana Jones.

Log No. _____

Date: ....

....
(hike/trail name)

Region/country: ....

(flag/symbol)

Start and end time: ....

Total duration: ....

Total distance: ....

Hike type: loop out and back one way day trip overnight

Elevation: ....

Fees: ....

Reception: ....

Facilities: ....
....

Other hikers: Many Some Few None

Temp: .... Wind: ....

Weather: ....

Companion(s): ....

117.

Equipment: ....

....

....

....

....

Route/trail names: ....

....

....

....

....

Notes: ....

....

....

....

....

....

....

....

(photo/drawing/notes)

- **Pros:** ....
- **Cons:** ....

Difficulty: ☆☆☆☆☆ **Overall rating:** ☆☆☆☆☆

Deepest Lake in the United States

Mount Mazama was a volcano that erupted and collapsed approximately 7,700 years ago, forming today's hiking destination — Crater Lake, the deepest lake in the United States.

Famous for its beautiful, deep blue hue, the lake doesn't have any external inlets of water — it all comes from rain or snow.

Log No. _____

Date: ....

....
(hike/trail name)

Region/country: ....

(flag/symbol)

Start and end time: .... | ....

Total duration: ....

Total distance: ....

Hike type: ↻ loop   ⇄ out and back   → one way   ☀ day trip   ⛺ overnight   ....

Elevation: ....

Fees: ....

Reception: ....

Facilities: ....

....

Other hikers:

- Many
- Some
- Few
- None

Temp: ....   Wind: ....

Weather: ....

Companion(s): ....

121.

Equipment: ....
....
....
....
....

Route/trail names: ....
....
....
....
....

Notes: ....
....
....
....
....
....
....
....
....

(photo/drawing/notes)

- Pros: ....
- Cons: ....

Difficulty: ☆☆☆☆☆　　Overall rating: ☆☆☆☆☆

© **Classic Publishing**

Made in the USA
Columbia, SC
01 July 2025

60209022R00070